MY FIRST JOKES AND RIDDLES

Quick, Call Me a Taxi!

by Judy Ziegler

GALLERY BOOKS
An Imprint of W. H. Smith Publishers Inc.
112 Madison Avenue
New York City 10016

An RGA Book

Copyright © 1991 by RGA Publishing Group, Inc.
This edition published in 1991 by Gallery Books,
an imprint of W.H. Smith Publishers, Inc., 112 Madison Avenue,
New York, New York 10016
Manufactured in the United States of America
Gallery Books are available for bulk purchase for sales promotions
and premium use. For details write or telephone the Manager of
Special Sales, W.H. Smith Publishers, Inc., 112 Madison Avenue,
New York, New York 10016. (212) 532-6600

ISBN 0-8317-6296-9

What looks like half a grapefruit?

The other half.

What kept the skunk from running out of the room?

The door.

Why was the policeman under a blanket?

He was an undercover cop.

Did you hear about the octopus who got hit
in the face with a pie?

He was octi-pied.

What do cows read?

They read the daily moos-paper.

What kind of bow can't be untied?

A rainbow.

Why did the horse wear two pairs of pants when he played golf?

In case he got a hole-in-one!

Why did the gorillas close their law firm?

Because all they got was monkey business.

What causes trees to be so noisy?

Their bark.

What did the beaver say when the raccoon told him, "You have your shoes on the wrong feet"?

"No, I don't. These are my feet!"

What do you call a dirty deer who crosses
the street twice?

What do pigs write letters with?

Pig pens.

What did the little chair say to the big chair?

What do you do if you swallow a roll of film?

Wait to see what develops!

Why do penguins take baths in tide?

Because it's too cold out-tide.

How do you send messages to fish?

Drop them a line.

A sick monkey.

Why did the crow need a phone?

He wanted to make a long-distance caw.

What has four wheels and flies?

A garbage truck.

Why is tennis so noisy?

Because someone is always raising a racket.

Why do bees have sticky hair?

Because they use honey combs.

What kind of key won't open a door?

Why did the goat sleep with a banana skin?

He wanted to slip out of bed in the morning.